Prophetess Kathryn Summers is a passionate worshipper who lives close to the heart of the Father. I've known for her more than 25 years, and I know no one more qualified to write this important message to the body of Christ. We've travelled the nations of the earth together teaching, preaching, and prophesying to lost and broken people. I've personally witnessed the resurrection power of God in her songs bring life, healing, and deliverance to everyone in the room. Prophetess Kathy embodies the power of prophetic worship—the songs sung by her bring heaven to earth causing an eternal weight of glory to fill a room. She is a true Chenaniah. The prophetic anointing on her life creates an atmosphere where God is enthroned and miracles are released. The wisdom shared in this book will be a catalyst to change the expression of the music industry as we know it.

Michelle McClain Walters
Author of *Prophetic Advantage*,
Esther Anointing, and *Hannah Anointing*

SOUNDS
THAT CHANGE
ATMOSPHERES,
RELEASE GLORY,
AND USHER IN
MIRACLES

THE DYNAMICS OF

Prophetic Worship

KATHRYN SUMMERS

DESTINY IMAGE® PUBLISHERS, INC.

P.O. Box 310, Shippensburg, PA 17257-0310

"Promoting Inspired Lives."

This book and all other Destiny Image and Destiny Image Fiction books are available at Christian bookstores and distributors worldwide.

Cover design by Eileen Rockwell
Interior design by Terry Clifton

For more information on foreign distributors, call 717-532-3040.

Reach us on the Internet: www.destinyimage.com.

ISBN 13 TP: 978-0-7684-4872-6
ISBN 13 eBook: 978-0-7684-4873-3
ISBN 13 HC: 978-0-7684-4875-7
ISBN 13 LP: 978-0-7684-4874-0

For Worldwide Distribution, Printed in the U.S.A.
1 2 3 4 5 6 7 8 / 23 22 21 20 19

DEDICATION

I dedicate this book to my late husband Romme Kelley, who now spends his time worshipping in the glory. My children Kia, Jerry, and Destiny, who mean the world to me. My grandchildren, because I see in them a different spirit set apart for the Lord, future worship leaders. And all true worshippers whose desire and mission are to bring glory to God.

ACKNOWLEDGMENTS

I acknowledge and greatly appreciate every prophetic person who spoke as God and caused the darkness to flee so that I could hear His loving voice and take my place in the Kingdom, for every song that was sung over me in the most obscure places. Your songs of the Lord sung over me became my peace. I am forever grateful.

I acknowledge Pastor John Eckhardt of Crusaders Church, Chicago, Illinois, for pouring his life into my life—equipping me for my future and the Kingdom. You are not just my spiritual father and apostle, I call you my friend! You have shared your family with my family and have encouraged us to keep blessing the Lord in His presence. I thank you for trusting me to lead the people in worship and doors you opened that took me around the world. You have been there from the beginning of my journey to worship the King of kings and the Lord of lords. Your example led me here to write it. Thank you!

Crusaders Church, I love you. You are slice of Heaven for all who come and fellowship with you and make you their home. You are my family because you belong to God and me. To all my special friends and mentors, you know who you are. I will never be same because you love me. Thank you!

CONTENTS

FOREWORD

*T*here is a new generation of believers being awakened to prophetic worship. Kathryn Summers Kelley is a vanguard in awakening this generation. Kathryn has a burning passion to see psalmists, minstrels, and worshippers move in the power of the Holy Spirit in worship. She has been a strong worship leader for many years, and she has operated in the prophetic anointing as long as I have known her.

I am so excited that she has written this book on prophetic worship. There is a new wave of revelation coming forth with the resurgence of prophetic worship. This book provides insight on the importance of prophecy in worship, and will stir psalmists, minstrels, and worship leaders to arise and fulfill their callings to usher people into the presence of God.

I have personally drawn from the insight that Kathryn offers on the subject of worship. She has helped me as a pastor gain more understanding of the power of prophetic worship, and why it is vital to the strength of local churches. Kathryn has also been instrumental in imparting to many emerging psalmists and minstrels. Her sensitivity to the Holy Spirit in worship has been a great blessing to our local assembly.

Worship was always the goal of the ages. The Father seeks worshippers. Worship must be done in Spirit and in truth. God has called the nations to worship, and every generation is required to worship. The Holy Spirit is our Helper in worship. We depend on His leading and anointing to give what the Lord requires. This cannot be done in the flesh—it can only be accomplished in the Spirit.

Prophecy, spontaneous songs, new songs, and new sounds are important if we are to experience the new thing that God desires to do in our lives. Worshipping with prophetic people is always refreshing and revelatory. Prophetic worship causes the heavens to be opened and the glory of God to manifest in our midst.

We need anointed psalmists and minstrels in every assembly. We need the spirit of prophecy, and we need to be activated prophetically in order to flow in the river of God. We are now ministering in the legacy of David, Chenaniah, Asaph, Heman, Jeduthun, and other Levites. This book will help you understand what prophetic worship is, and why we need to move in it consistently.

The truths in this book will set you free. Freedom from the limitations of our incorrect or lack of teaching will be broken. Knowledge and wisdom are important if you desire to minister to the Lord. We are learning more and more on this important subject. The more we teach and learn, the more we will experience the glory of the Lord.

Be blessed as you read this book, and may the Lord give you understanding in all things.

JOHN ECKHARDT
Overseer of Crusaders Ministries
Chicago, Illinois, USA

INTRODUCTION

The Dynamics of Prophetic Worship is filled with revelation, insight, and testimonies that help believers understand their role as prophetic worshippers. This book will create a desire in you to see God in a fresh, new way and realize that it's God's desire for His people to break out into the deep call He has placed in our hearts, before we were formed in our mother's womb.

God reveals Himself to those who seek after Him. There is so much more He wants the Church to know concerning His prophetic minstrels and psalmists. God is raising up a prophetic, creative, innovative, and bold army of believers in this hour. Take your place and become the true wo rshipper God has called you to be—to worship God prophetically!

Chapter 1

THE UNTAPPED POWER OF MUSIC

Music's Origin

We all have preferences regarding just about everything that I can think of. Music may be at the top of your list or at least close to the top. Do you prefer Classic, Contemporary Christian, Rhythm and Blues, Country? Music is one of the most complex art forms that can only be judged individually—as everyone has their own opinion. It is wonderfully diverse! What music is to my ears can be noise to another.

We cannot argue the fact that music is like the saying, "Beauty is in the eye of the beholder." I would endeavor to say that perception and interpretation alone are insufficient ways to understand the depth of what we call music and what we have been so blessed to enjoy. Music is the backdrop of humanity; and God forbid if the music would ever stop!

The Merriam-Webster Dictionary defines music this way: The science or art of ordering tones or sounds in succession, in combination, and in temporal relationships to produce a composition. Vocal, instrumental, or mechanical sounds having rhythm, melody, or harmony.

Rhythm, melody, and harmony are perhaps the only understanding of the majority of people who have experienced music. People tend to sum up music into two categories—good or bad. This is the easiest way to avoid getting into the depth and complexity what music really is.

The dictionary definition of music is very good, but I want to look further into the origination of music. Anyone one who believes in God believes that God created the heavens and the earth, our world, and will agree that God created music—that it came from within Himself. In other words, music came out of God.

Kevin J. Conner, author of *The Tabernacle of David,* states that there should be no doubt as to the origin of music. Music either originated with God or the devil or man. Scripture revelation of music suggests that music originated in the heart of God (Ezekiel 28:13-14 KJV). Before humankind was created, and even before the angelic hosts were created, music was in the very being of God. What a powerful truth; the possibilities of this gift to mankind is endless.

Have you ever thought about how the film industry changed when music was added to help tell the story and to ensure the audience felt the right emotion? The art of influence. Why does music have such an effect on humanity? Could it be that music is part of our DNA? In fact, some geneticists believe that the patterns of music look like human DNA strands.

Music Comes from God

The Bible says humans are created in God's likeness and image (Genesis 1:26). Music comes from God. We have an ability to create music from within; music comes from the imagination of the composer and is manifested through melodies and harmonies.

In the book of Revelation, the twenty-four elders each have a harp and a bowl. The harps are music and the bowls are the prayers of the saints (Revelation 5:8). There is music on earth; and in Heaven, just think, music will be for eternity.

Music is constantly changing; it is reproduced repeatedly. I believe that humankind has a need to express what is deep within our human spirit—tones, melodies, and harmonies—and it must get out. Many people look at music as a form of art.

Music is in all of God's creation; listen to the birds sing, the whistling winds, and the great fish of the ocean. Each of God's creations has its own voice. Yes, music has a voice. We give music its voice when we add words and structure; however, structure is determined by the creator and variations of arrangements. This is a creative force that can change and take on another expression. The tricky part about music is that although it is composed by its producer, it is interpreted differently by the listener.

Not all music is good, bad, or godly, although many people look at it as a form of art. The problem is, certain musical compositions are nothing but arrangements of discord. Yes, some music can be interpreted as non-harmonic. Again, music was created from the heart of God—but it is defiled by satan and humans. Defilement breeds nothing but sin, rebellion, discord, destruction, and confusion.

The Bible speaks about the angelic host of angels that lucifer led in the worship of God, before his fall from Heaven. These angels were influenced by lucifer and rebelled against God (see Ezekiel 28:14-16; Isaiah 14:12). It is important to understand that satan's ability to compose music and his wisdom was not removed from him. I believe that music must be discerned by the Spirit of God. I often say that music never asks for your permission to invade your spirit.

> *Music never asks for your permission to invade your spirit.*

Every generation creates their own sound of music. One generation may even find another's preference annoying. To narrow music down to two agreeable points is that it can carry the sound of life or death. Music can be an aid to express the Spirit of God, humankind's fickle preferences, or satan's demonic influences over humankind.

In *The Tabernacle of David,* Conner states that music is neither moral or immoral. It's amoral. It is the *use* of music that makes it evil or good, destroying or edifying.

God has a plan for His music—to edify His children and to glorify Himself. Discerning the spirit behind the music we hear will help protect our spirits. One of the ways we can determine the spirit is through lyrical content. Scripture tells us that life and death is the power of the tongue: *"The tongue has the power of life and death..."* (Proverbs 18:21 NIV). So, listening closely to the lyrics of the song will usually provide the intent—uplifting or depressing, joyful or hateful.

We cannot control the secular music industry, but we *can* control what we will allow into our soul through our senses. Don't under estimate the influence of music. Expect that God is doing something new in the music dimension, while understanding that satan is capable of perverting music as well.

Gateway to Hell

Before I became a Christian, I was signed to a record label, composing music and singing in local clubs. One day one of the producers asked me to sing on a project he was working on for a rock band. I sat down at the mixing board and put the headphones over my ears. Almost immediately, I entered what I believe was hell, or a demonic prison that was structured like caves. I could hear screaming and could smell something so awful.

What I perceived very strongly—this was the place called fear. This encounter impacted all my senses. The next thing I did was take off the headphones and run out of the studio into the streets, with the producers running behind me. They thought I was having a bad drug trip. The only problem with that assumption—I was not using drugs at all. The music was a portal, or gateway, to another realm. I knew firsthand that this music was influenced by devil worshippers. The guys in the band were involved in the occult.

> *Music is influenced by the soul of the person composing it.*

Music is influenced by the soul of the person composing it. An individual's ideas and beliefs are portrayed through the music. The listeners, innocent unsuspecting victims, can be impacted by the nature of the music. The definition of the word "portal" means a doorway, gate, or entrance, especially a large and elaborate one. Synonyms include doorway, gateway, entrance, exit, opening. Believers must be aware of how easy it is to open their hearts, minds, and souls to the demonic through the music they listen to.

Because of this life-changing encounter that day, I became seriously circumspect about what kinds of music I chose to be involved in. It was a supernatural experience; and I began questioning myself, *How could something like that happen? I was just innocently listening to a piece of music, something harmless. How could music take a person into hell?* Without a doubt, I knew it was demonic.

The Prince of the Air

Ephesians 2:2 (AMP) says:

> *You were following the ways of this world [influenced by this present age], in accordance with the prince of the power of the air (Satan), the spirit who is now at work in the disobedient [the unbelieving, who fight against the purposes of God].*

Most people believe that the supernatural realm is the invisible realm where powers or unexplained things are happening—things that cannot be explained with human intellect. Satan is referred to as the prince of the air because he has power in this world and has influence over people. His domain is the air—which is all around us. Air is invisible and he operates from the invisible realm. The air above the earth, in the earth's atmosphere, is where the most influential communication networks operate. Radio, television, and satellite signals are streaming through the airways constantly, influencing people, cities, governments, and nations worldwide.

Music is also heard over the airways. Satan influences people through perverted music. Although he does not hold his place before God as the covering cherub anymore (Ezekiel 28:16), he is still in authority and has the power to influence music that is birthed from an unregenerate spirit.

> *The voice of the Lord will break the powers of music that keep people in the dark about the His glory.*

There are powers that desire to destroy humanity through music. Any music that is created is spiritual and has lasting effects on the body, mind, and spirit. It is like the air—you can't see it, but you can feel it within, and hear it. Music affects you—whether you desire it or not.

Ephesians 6:12 (NIV) says:

> *For our struggle is not against flesh and blood, but against the rulers, against the authorities, against the powers of this dark world and against the spiritual forces of evil in the heavenly realms.*

Get ready for something new in music. The voice of the Lord will break the powers and influences of music that have been created to keep humankind in the dark about the glory of the Lord. His will be revealed!

Chapter 2

WHAT IS PROPHETIC WORSHIP?

<hr>

Prophetic worship is the voice of God being released through believers as we praise and worship the Lord. We must make room for the voice of the Lord by yielding ourselves to the Holy Spirit in our private and public ministry unto the Lord. God is alive and His voice is strong and mighty. Let our praise and worship glorify His name.

When we worship God in spirit and in truth, His Spirit helps us. Another way to put it—His Spirit quickens us and stirs up a spontaneous flow of genuine worship to our God. Spontaneous worship often leads us into another place in worship that is not organized—and new songs and music pour from the hearts of the worshippers.

Keep in mind that as we commune with God, He responds to us. It is God's Spirit who dwells in us, which gives us a prophetic voice.

Think about the creative nature of God and all His creation. The natural mind cannot comprehend the power and wisdom that it took just to create one grain of dirt. Yet God formed Adam from the soil of the earth and then breathed life into him. Adam and Eve walked in harmony with their heavenly Father—they communicated with Him intimately. It is important to understand that we should all desire to hear and obey the voice of the Lord. In fact, the Word of God states that we should covet to prophesy:

> *Wherefore, brethren, **covet to prophesy**, and forbid not to speak in tongues. Let all things be done decently and in order* (1 Corinthians 14:39-40 KJV).

*Therefore, my brothers and sisters, **be eager to prophesy**, and do not forbid speaking in tongues. But everything should be done in a fitting and orderly way* (1 Corinthians 14:39-40 NIV).

The word "covet" means to wish for earnestly; to desire. To want something, that you don't have, very badly. This is one time the word of God encourages us to covet something. Many believers are now starting to realize that God still speaks as He did to the prophets of the Old Testament.

Prophetic worship does not require us to have the office of the prophet to release His voice.

God Desires Prophetic People

And afterward, I will pour out my Spirit on all people. Your sons and daughters will prophesy, your old men will dream dreams, your young men will see visions (Joel 2:28 NIV).

*For **you can all prophesy** in turn so that everyone may be instructed and encouraged* (1 Corinthians 14:31 NIV).

So, it's good to say that this is something that God desires for us all to learn how to be instructed and encouraged. When the worshippers gather in the name of Jesus, to worship Him in spirit and truth, we must yield to the Holy Spirit and make room to hear and release what God is saying. If you are born again, you can prophetically worship God. You have the testimony of Jesus, which is the spirit of prophecy.

Revelation 19:10 says:

> *At this I fell at his feet to worship him. But he said to me, "Don't do that! I am a fellow servant with you and with your brothers and sisters who hold to **the testimony of Jesus**. Worship God! For it is the **Spirit of prophecy** who bears testimony to Jesus."*

We have the Spirit of God in us who is the Holy Spirit and He will help us to worship God. The prophetic anointing is given to all of God's Spirit-filled believers. It is a gift from God. We must never separate worship and the prophetic as we learn more and desire more of God—keep in mind that worship and the prophetic go hand in hand.

Simply Confounded

I am reminded of the first time I heard a woman sing a song of the Lord. I was amazed. And to be very honest, she did not have the best singing voice. Yet I was simply confounded by what I heard and felt.

The words touched my life deeply to the point that I wanted to hear more of this mystery. You see, I was not a Christian at that time. I tell you, though, this sound messed me up. I was convicted and things began to change.

I had heard beautiful singing before, but nothing like this. It affected me so much that I could not sing the same songs I was singing at that time in my life. During that time, I was singing in local clubs in Chicago and opening for a well-known artist. But upon meeting this prophetic worshipper, I could no longer produce, and working on secular music became very difficult. I was changing!

I was drawn into something deeper and spiritual. What I discovered was that only a born-again believer can sing a new song!

Covet to Prophesy

I coveted to prophesy. This is a supernatural provoking of the Spirit of God that brings transformation. My genuine response was not to sing. I wanted to worship the God who saves. I remember saying, "Lord, all I want to do is to worship You."

Upon my introduction to the Kingdom of God, for the first time I felt alive. The next thing I said is, "Lord, if there is anything I could do for You, please let me prophesy!" I came alive and wanted to bless others the same way that He used this woman to bless me. The song of the Lord brings the breath of God into a person's life. God's Word is alive and will quicken the mortal body and the soul.

The Bible declares that God breathed upon Adam and he became a living soul. Although I was living, my soul was dead to Christ. When we accept Christ as our Lord and Savior, His Spirit will dwell in us.

> *So it is written: "The first man Adam became a living being"; the last Adam, a life-giving spirit* (1 Corinthians 15:45 NIV).

> *So it is written [in Scripture], the first man Adam, became a living soul* (an individual)*; the last Adam* (Christ) *became a life-giving spirit [restoring the dead to life]* (1 Corinthians 15:45 AMP).

Prophetic worship is God's plan for us. It fills us with His Spirit, giving life to things that are dead. The best part is that everyone can worship prophetically. When we sing or speak God's word over someone's life, we release the breath of God. Yes, prophetic singing releases the very breath of God. Another way to put it is born-again believers can all breathe life into our congregational worship—into each other for the glory of God. New songs release new things.

God wants to daily revive our souls with His breath.

Can you imagine what it was like for Adam and Eve to walk, talk, commune, and worship God the Father in the cool of the day in the beautiful Garden of Eden? When God breathed into Adam, the Bible says he became a living soul. God's voice is His presence. God wants to daily revive our souls with His breath. When we walk with Him and allow His voice to be released, life is restored.

When Adam sinned, he lost his ability to stay in that place. The moment that God came to him and asked where he was, Adam replied that he was hiding because he was afraid and naked.

> And **they heard the voice of the Lord God**
> *walking in the garden in the cool of the day:*
> *and Adam and his wife hid themselves from*
> *the presence of the Lord God amongst the trees*
> *of the garden* (Genesis 3:8 KJV).

Take note that God came to the same place with Adam as He had previously. Adam was the one hiding—because sin separates us from God. Notice that Adam and Eve were afraid, as they heard the voice of God.

The voice of the Lord is still speaking in the midst of chaos and sin. God wants to restore His voice to His people so that we may know Him. We must desire God's presence more than anything else. His voice is His presence! God's voice has many expressions of His glory. His presence brings glory to dark places.

The Voice of the Lord

> **The voice of the Lord** *is upon the waters; the*
> *God of glory thunders; the Lord is over many*
> *waters.* **The voice of the Lord** *is powerful;*
> *the voice of the Lord is full of majesty.* **The**

voice of the Lord breaks the cedars; yes, the
Lord breaks in pieces the cedars of Lebanon.
The voice of the Lord rakes flames of fire
(lightning) (Psalm 29:3-5,7 AMP).

Now that we know that God's voice is His presence, we
can see how powerful His presence is and how much we
need to cry out for His glory like Moses did. The Bible
says that Moses cried out for God to show him His glory.
The Lord answered Moses by speaking to him from a
burning bush.

*Now Moses was tending the flock of Jethro his
father-in-law, the priest of Midian, and he led
the flock to the far side of the wilderness and
came to Horeb, the mountain of God. There
the angel of **the Lord appeared to him in
flames of fire** from within a bush. Moses saw
that though the bush was on fire it did not burn
up. So Moses thought, "I will go over and see
this strange sight—why the bush does not burn
up." When the Lord saw that he had gone over
to look, God called to him from within the
bush, "Moses! Moses!" And Moses said, "Here I
am" (Exodus 3:1-4 NIV).*

So many Christians are afraid of the flames, because of sin and disobedience. We must understand that God's voice is our covering and defense against any lie or anything that can harm us. The voice of the Lord divides the flames. The very flames that were burning in the bush are the same flames that will protect you from your enemies. Moses saw a bush that wasn't consumed by the very flames that God spoke to him from. Then God brought Moses to a cleft in a rock to protect and cover him so that Moses could see his goodness. So that Moses could see His glory! (Exodus 33:22.)

Prophetic worship releases the glory of God. The word "glory" in Hebrew is *kabod,* which means heavy and weighty. God likes to release His weighty presence. There are times when God's *kabod* is strong in prophetic worship. A person can sense it and it's almost impossible to go on in the service. I imagined this was what it was like in the tabernacle of David. They worshipped around the clock. Twenty-four hours a day for forty years. Israel was a strong, influential nation and its glory could not be matched.

Prophetic Worship Dynamics

There are many dynamics to prophetic worship. The culture that prophetic people live in is supernatural. I have never experienced a boring moment in my life since I met our prophetic God.

Prophetic worship is not about the songs we sing. The songs we sing are a result of our spontaneous, prophetic nature and desire to respond to God who is very much alive and desires to commune with us.

I have asked many friends and family members what it was like for them the first time they visited my local church. Two words to sum up their responses—glorious and supernatural. Many people told me that they were turned into another person. One leader told me that it felt like the Bible opened up to him like a major movie playing on a large screen—except it was real. Wow!

Prophetic people carry a tangible anointing. I remember my own children prophesying and blessing my soul. I keep their anointing activated by asking them if they have a word for mommy. Prophetic people need to keep activated, ensuring they are blessing people around them with the glory of the Lord.

Chapter 3

THE PROPHETIC ANOINTING AND WORSHIP

*P*rophetic worship will turn you into a different person. You may consider that a strong statement, but I believe it's true. For example, consider this passage from First Samuel 10:

> *After that you [Saul] will go to Gibeah of God, where there is a Philistine outpost. As you*

*approach the town, **you will meet a procession of prophets** coming down from the high place with lyres, timbrels, pipes and harps being played before them, and they will be prophesying. **The Spirit of the Lord will come powerfully upon you**, and you will prophesy with them; and **you will be changed into a different person*** (1 Samuel 10:5-6 NIV).

Worshipping with the prophets activated a prophetic anointing in Saul that changed his nature and changed him into a different man. The Spirit of the Lord came upon him and he was empowered! I believe that worship and prophecy go hand in hand, now add *empowerment* to the equation and it becomes supernatural. Saul is encouraged by Samuel to serve God with his gift.

Try to imagine what it would be like if believers were all changed into other people like Saul. We all can prophesy. The level of glory will be astounding. Saul was not just activated. He was empowered to serve God.

The Spirit of prophecy is God's Spirit in us—the Holy Spirit, working to help us so we can help others.

Samuel told Saul that it was a sign that God was with him.

New Order of Worship

King David established a new order of worship—something that had never been done before in Israel. Before David brought the Ark of the Covenant to Jerusalem, it was restricted to the Holy of Holies in the tent of meeting and only the priest had access. Now, all Israel could come to this new place of worship and have access to God's glory. In fact, this model is considered by scholars to be a New Testament covenant worship in an Old Covenant era.

> *Wearing a linen ephod, David was dancing before the Lord with all his might, while he and all Israel were bringing up the ark of the Lord with shouts and the sound of trumpets. …They brought the ark of the Lord and set it in its place inside the tent that David had pitched for it, and David sacrificed burnt offerings and fellowship offerings before the Lord. After he had finished sacrificing the burnt offerings and fellowship offerings, he blessed*

> *the people in the name of the Lord Almighty*
> (2 Samuel 6:14,17-18 NIV).

David brought the Ark of God to himself and created a place where all people could experience God's glory. He established a dwelling place for all Jerusalem in his generation, changing the world forever. He focused on God with all his might.

> *Besides, in my devotion to the temple of my God I now give my personal treasures of gold and silver for the temple of my God, over and above everything I have provided for this holy temple* (1 Chronicles 29:3 NIV).

What a glorious time it was for all Israel. David established singers and minstrels to minister to the Lord for twenty-four hours a day, seven days a week. They all had shifts, specific times when they would worship God in the temple of the Lord. This was joyful praise and worship unto God. Consider those who didn't know the God of Israel who were listening to this extravagant and beautiful praise. As Israel lifted their praises to God, people were drawn to the Lord and were added to the Kingdom.

> *David, together with the commanders of the army, set apart some of the **sons of Asaph,***

> ***Heman and Jeduthun*** *for the **ministry of prophesying, accompanied by harps, lyres and cymbals**. Here is the list of the men who performed this service ...All these men were under the supervision of their father for **the music of the temple of the Lord**, with **cymbals, lyres and harps**, for the ministry at the house of God. Asaph, Jeduthun and Heman were under the supervision of the king. Along with their relatives—all of them **trained and skilled in music for the Lord**—they numbered 288. Young and old alike, teacher as well as student, cast lots for their duties* (1 Chronicles 25:1,6-8 NIV).

I believe that during David's reign and the establishment of prophesying minstrels and psalmists, he was successful in expanding the Kingdom. They sang new songs and prophesied on their instruments. This was glorious in the sight of God. Today's church can experience this same kind of glory, or greater.

It is important to notice that the men mentioned in First Chronicles 25 were the king's seers and prophesied according to the commandment of David. The sons shared the responsibilities of the service of worship unto the Lord. This model is exactly what is necessary for today's worship ministers. Having the next generation trained to worship is important to the Father. I believe those who follow this pattern will see the hand of God upon their lives.

It is important for us today to have prophets involved in praise and worship. Asaph, Jeduthun, and Heman were prophets who served as chief worship leaders in the tabernacle of David. They did not just play instruments. They gave themselves to the study of the Word and were separated unto God for ministry. I believe these prophets dealt with Israel's issues through their prophetic expression in music.

In apostle John Eckhardt's book, *Worshiping with the Prophets,* he states that musicians by nature are very perceptive. Prophets make great worship leaders and if you are not worshipping with the prophets, then you are not experiencing true worship. Prophets help open the door for the King of Glory to come in.

First Chronicles 15:22 states that Chenaniah, the prince of the Levites, *"presided in prophecy, because he had understanding"* (Jubilee Bible 2000). Chenaniah was also a prophet. He can be described as the supervisor of the songs of the Lord. Some call him the master of song. He carried the burden of songs of the Lord. Prophets carried the burden and heart of God.

According to *The Worshiper's Topical Bible and Worshiping with the Prophets,* the word "master" means chief leader or prince; "song" is the Hebrew word *massa* meaning a burden, utterance oracle or prophecy.

Chenaniah instructed the singers as to the direction the Spirit of God was leading. Chenaniah was a man of wisdom and understanding. He is the planter for the Lord. His name means: established by God, preparation or disposition, or strength, of the Lord. The anointing of Chenaniah is needed in praise and worship.

Leaders must recognize that the ministry of the prophets is not limited to speaking prophetic words only. I believe that today's prophetic people have only touched the surface in this type of ministry. God desires for all to have the Spirit of prophecy operating in their lives.

> *God desires for all to have the Spirit of prophecy operating in their lives.*

All believers should carry the burden of the heart and mind of God in every aspect of life. One of the ways that God's glory can be revealed is through the anointing of prophecy. Christ is revealed. I have seen many believers transformed through the ministry of the prophets. Prophets help build the Church through the perfecting of saints. Every one of us are to be doing the work of ministry.

> *But Moses replied, "Are you jealous for my sake? I wish that all the Lord's people were prophets and that the Lord would put his Spirit on them!"* (Numbers 11:29 NIV)

Moses simply desired that all the people would be endowed with the power of God. This is the glory! They would be empowered to whatever was needed; they could help themselves, and this would in fact expand the Kingdom.

Bring Me a Minstrel!

I love and appreciate the ministry of the minstrel—those who sing and play instruments. I am privileged to have ministered with some of the most talented men and women of God. They can easily be misunderstood and also the most tolerated regardless of their lifestyle. Sometimes minstrels appear in the forefront of the church and are segregated at the same time from the congregation. Many people often treat them like celebrities because they see them on the stage and everything they do is highlighted.

Consider the stage, lights, and cameras if your local congregation has all the latest technical enhancements in providing you with a contemporary worship experience in the service. Keep this in mind as you look at the minstrels. True worship does not need music. We are admonished in the Word of God to make melody in our hearts to God: *"Speaking to yourselves in psalms and hymns and spiritual songs, singing and making melody in your heart to the Lord"* (Ephesians 5:19 KJV). We use musical instruments to help express our heartfelt worship to the Lord in art form.

True worship is in spirit and truth.

True worship is in spirit and truth. This is what the Father seeks. Worship comes from the heart and spirit of a man. It is spiritual. God is Spirit! I believe to qualify as a true minstrel you must first be a worshipper, connected to God. I have met many talented musicians but nothing inspired me more than an anointed minstrel who ministered unto the Lord.

> *But the hour is coming, and now is, when the* **true worshipers will worship the Father in spirit and truth; for the Father is seeking such to worship Him.** **God is Spirit**, *and those who worship Him must worship in spirit and truth* (John 4:23-24).

God loves music. Yes, He does. He created anointed music in Heaven and on earth. Lucifer, the covering cherub, was fashioned with every precious stone—sardius, topaz, diamond, beryl, onyx, jasper, sapphire, emerald, carbuncle, and gold. Tabrets and pipes were also part of his makeup (Ezekiel 28:13 KJV). He offered praise and worship to the Lord.

God equipped lucifer with everything he needed to offer up glorious praise—but his gift became corrupted with pride. What was revealed to lucifer was not for himself, it was for God. What a lesson we can learn from him! We were created *by* God *for* God—to praise God, not ourselves.

Prophetic people do not allow what is revealed to them to become stumbling blocks for others. It is to the glory of God that we know what we know. I can imagine the prophetic ministry of this covering cherub. I don't see a lot of old dead songs. (Just saying. Think about it.)

Minstrels Uncover Mysteries

Elisha the prophet is sought after to give a word from the Lord as to what ought to be done on behalf of three kings who banded together against Moab. However, he would do so because of Jehoshaphat the king of Judah. Elisha was not in the best frame of mind because of his holy indignation of an unholy and idolatrous king.

> *But now bring me a minstrel [musician]. And it came to pass, when the minstrel played, that the hand of the Lord came upon him* (2 Kings 3:15 KJV).

Elisha is the prophet with a double-portion anointing. Surely he was anointed enough to hear from God, so it would seem; but he is human and filled with godly rage against lawlessness. He needed help, so he asked for a musician!

The anointed minstrel helped Elisha clear his mind and get the mind of God. Elisha clearly did not prophesy out of his emotions. I believe that without the help of the minstrel, this would have been difficult for him. Minstrels have a unique ability to uncover mysteries. As it says in Psalm 49:4 (NIV), *"I will turn my ear to a proverb; with the harp I will expound my riddle."* The New King James Version says, *"I will incline my ear to a proverb; I will disclose my dark saying on the harp."* This means to solve the riddle, to get understanding, and or receive wisdom.

The minstrel made things very clear for the prophet. God's hand could now work in Elisha.

When we call for prophetic minstrels today, we understand the grace on their lives. Many of the minstrels are

Submit your gift to God.

prophetic and filled with the Spirit of God. I often tell the minstrels, "You are not playing for me, we are ministering to the Lord together. I will follow you and you will follow with me as we flow together. It's like a river's current that can change; and wherever the river goes, we flow."

Minstrels have the ability to tap into the supernatural realms. Music is a doorway to the supernatural. Therefore, it is important to submit your gift to God. Lucifer took what God gave him for his own selfish gain, which is disobedience, vanity, and pride and caused him to be cast down from Heaven, forfeiting his call and rightful place of rule. This deceitful spirit is influencing the ungodly music we hear today. Music takes on the spirit of the influencer. Ask yourself who influences the music that you play and or listen to—the Holy Spirit or an evil spirit.

I believe David was one of the greatest minstrels who ever lived and ministered before the Lord. We can glean this perspective from his preparations and knowing that David is a man after God's on heart. He began to worship and develop his relationship with God while tending his father's sheep. He also learned and became skilled under the teaching and training in Samuel's school of the prophet.

David was trained and submitted to authority. Sometimes minstrels do not believe they need training. But, gifting alone is not enough. Submitting to authority protects minstrels from satan's traps. Also, submission to the proper authority releases the minstrels to operate fully in their own authority.

We cannot ignore the incredible success that David walked in. As king, he appointed minstrel teams and commanded them to prophesy on their instruments. They were always under governmental authority. This is a major key to protecting the anointing and the vessel God is using. We do not desire to cap anyone's gift. We understand the importance of living a lifestyle pleasing to God and protecting the congregation. Leaders cannot be afraid of disciplining minstrels. This will save their lives and preserve the anointing.

Holy Spirit-breathed music by minstrels change people—because it is alive by the Spirit of the living God. The following are some things to consider about anointed minstrels.

Anointed minstrels can:

- Drive out evil spirits

- Ease mental illness

- Prophesy day and night

- Help heal disease

- Transcend the normal

- Reset the mind, body, and spirit

- Tap into the supernatural realm

Let's look at some Scriptures that confirm these statements.

David is called upon to aid Saul in his mental illness: *"And so it was, whenever the spirit from God was upon Saul, that David would take a harp and play it with his hand. Then Saul would become refreshed and well, and the distressing spirit would depart from him"* (1 Samuel 16:23).

King David raised up the greatest military music bands in his time. These were a company of minstrels who prophesied day and night (1 Chronicles 25).

Anointed music can help heal diseases. Anointed music, inspired by God, transcends the normal and can operate outside of an earthly realm and affect everything in its environment. Scientists believe that music affects everything, including the human brain.

When we address the body and its response to the anointing, we believe that it is the anointing that destroys yokes of bondages, sin, and sickness. The Lord will sing over His people and quiet us with love. Many believers who are under the bondage of disease may simply have a demon, spirit of bitterness, etc.

> *It shall come to pass in that day that his burden will be taken away from your shoulder, and his yoke from your neck, and the yoke will be destroyed because of the anointing oil* (Isaiah 10:27).

The Lord your God in your midst, the Mighty One, will save; He will rejoice over you with gladness, He will quiet you with His love, He will rejoice over you with singing (Zephaniah 3:17).

Music can be like a reset button, for the brain, heart and mind. Elisha was reset to hear God.

Second Kings 3:15 says:

"But now bring me a musician" Then it happened, when the musician played, that the hand of the Lord came upon him.

Chapter 4

A NEW SONG

We are commanded to *"sing to the Lord a new song."* God likes new songs and new things. There is power released when we sing new songs to God.

> **Sing to the Lord a new song; sing to the Lord,** *all the earth.* **Sing to the Lord***, praise his name; proclaim his salvation day after day* (Psalm 96:1-2 NIV).

God's name will be made known in our praise. As we sing new songs, in praise and worship, what seems ordinary becomes extraordinary moments when God reveals the secrets of our hearts. God wants the whole earth to come to the place of true worship. The Father seeks true worshippers. He draws us by His Spirit.

Prophetic singing to the Lord is not just your A and B song selection for the worship service. It is unrehearsed songs that spring from the heart of the worshipper. Prophetic people love the presence of the Lord; they live to hear His voice in every part of their lives. They know that His voice will release His glory.

> *Moreover David and the captains of the army separated for the service some of the sons of Asaph, of Heman, and of Jeduthun,* **who should prophesy with harps, stringed instruments, and cymbals.** *And the number of the skilled men performing their service was* (1 Chronicles 25:1).

There is an order to the kind of worship that the Father seeks after. As you read previously, we are commanded to *worship the Father in spirit and in truth*. The captains of the worship teams were commanded by the king to prophesy on their instruments. They were not just playing music or just any song—they yielded themselves to the Spirit of prophecy.

The minstrels, the musicians, did not just show up because it was their turn to play. Although they were commanded by the king, they were worshippers. Worship God for the testimony of Jesus is the Spirit of prophecy. Remember Saul coming into the company of prophets worshipping on instruments? It was the worship that brought about the change—God Himself prophesying upon the instruments.

When the minstrels worshipped God, the spirit of prophecy came upon them. What makes it difficult for minstrels to prophesy on the instruments is the lack of intimacy with God. Unfortunately, we have many minstrels who are gifted but lack the power of God and His presence.

The worship King David established would set the tone for how we worship God today. God liked the way David worshipped. David made room for the voice of the Lord through musical expressions and singing the song of the Lord. This level of creativity keeps our praise and worship alive. God likes to be in the midst of His people. God said that David was a man after His own heart. I believe we must be people like David. Davidic worship is a pattern that is eternal and generational. David brought Heaven to earth. Can you imagine how the culture began to shift in his day? I have no doubt it was like living in a supernatural realm.

Like David, we must shift and break away from our ritualistic worship and allow the Spirit of prophecy to invade our world with a new song and come alive to the God of our future, who from the beginning wanted to have a face-to-face relationship with His children.

Prophesying on instruments was something new in worship. The song of the Lord was not ministered by way of singing only, but also by those who played instruments. If we are going to follow the Davidic pattern for worship, we must incorporate this model of ministry.

Today many singers and minstrels have not been taught that it is God's desire for them to prophesy in song and on instruments. They have left it up to the prophets to speak, not realizing that David had many prophets and prophetic people who were part of the worship ministry.

The Song of the Lord

I doubt it could be known how many songs have been sung from the beginning of time. We learn to sing as children—all children around the world sing, but the tunes and instruments vary. Some believe that babies sing in the womb. Ask anyone who desires to be a famous singer how long they have been singing. Nine times out of ten they say they have been singing for as long as they can remember, or since they were a young child. No matter what culture or ethnic background, singing is universal, as common as the sound of music.

Singing is part of who God created us to be. My earliest memory of singing is when I was between eight and ten years old. My babysitter heard me singing a song my father would sing from a record he played continually throughout the house. The sitter would bring people to hear me sing. I didn't think it was that big of a deal because singing was something I always did. It was part of me—the way I lived.

Growing up, my family did not attend church and there was not much singing about Jesus. My siblings and I would attend church with the babysitter; she was the choir director. We went to many rehearsals with her. I could tell there was a difference between the music my father sang and the music the choir sang. Believe it or not, though, it all felt the same.

The song of the Lord changed my life forever! I have been exposed to all kinds of music over my lifetime, and was once signed to a record label. I was an opening act for people who were established in the industry—but there was nothing like the song of the Lord!

My father sang songs about life and the choir sang songs *about* Jesus. But nobody was singing *to* Him. I didn't hear a new song of the Lord in church. I heard this new song while I was standing at a bus stop waiting for the bus to arrive. A woman walked up to me and asked if she could share something with me. I said sure—and her song saved my life! I was captivated, not knowing the magnitude of the change that was about to happen to my life.

The song she sang from the Lord began to tear down the foundations of darkness in my life and started the process that has brought me to this very page. It was more than the sound of her voice, it was the Spirit of the words—which was the voice of the Lord.

> ***The Lord your God in your midst***, *the Mighty One, will save; He will rejoice over you with gladness, He will quiet you with His love,* ***He will rejoice over you with singing*** (Zephaniah 3:17).

God came to me in a human voice and spirit and sang over me and brought hope for my soul. From that time forward, I could not function as the singer I was before. I was being turned around, literally!

Thank God we exchanged phone numbers. One song was not enough. I was scared, but I kept calling her. I didn't know then that this woman was introducing me to true worship and the Father was fighting for me in every song she sang to me and in every prayer she prayed for me. This was indeed sweet fellowship. I was being transformed! Yes!

God sings over us, sometimes through other people. This kind of singing did more than just calm my nerves or rock me to sleep like a child's nursery rhyme. My eyes began to open. My heart began to long for the God who loved me so much. I wanted to worship Him; and somehow I understood that this woman was a worshipper and that she was worshipping Jesus, her Savior. I desired to be a worshipper more than I wanted to be a singer—and I hoped that if God would ever use me, I wanted to be a blessing to people like this woman was to me.

God sang over me and brought hope for my soul.

When I look back on my life as a singer before I became a believer, it was very clear to me that I was a woman singing without a purpose. None of the songs I was singing brought real conviction within me or any lasting change to anyone who heard me sing. It was just entertainment. Like Saul, though, I came into the company of worshipping prophets and was changed into another person, a different person who wanted to be a blessing to others. The Bible says they were worshipping, prophesying, and playing instruments. Everyone was prophesying. I was now part of the company of prophets!

If you have ever doubted your ability to sing the song of the Lord, today is the day you stop doubting. First, if you are a Spirit-filled believer, get ready. You are on your way to becoming all that God intended.

Chapter 5

THE SONG OF THE LORD

*L*et's look at King David, the man who wrote most of the Psalms. David is a man after God's own heart and his devotion to God is relentless in his pursuit to dwell in God's presence always. David wrote:

> *One thing I have asked of the Lord, and that I will seek: that I may dwell in the house of the Lord [in His presence] all the days of my life,*

> *to gaze upon the beauty [the delightful loveli-*
> *ness and majestic grandeur] of the Lord and*
> *to meditate in His temple* (Psalm 27:4 AMP).

When we pursue God with our whole heart, it will not be hard for us to respond to Him with singing and prophesying. Ephesians 5:19 (AMP) says, *"Speak to one another in psalms and hymns and spiritual songs, [offering praise by] singing and making melody in your heart to the Lord."*

Singing and making melody in your heart to Lord is a sweet tune sung out of your love—the place where your affections are focused. Ask yourself, *Is Jesus my love focus?* The heart sings out to the Lord. Remember, *"...Out of the abundance of the heart the mouth speaks"* (Matthew 12:34).

Isaiah 51:3 says:

> *For the Lord will comfort Zion, He will comfort*
> *all her waste places; He will make her wilder-*
> *ness like Eden, and her desert like the garden of*
> *the Lord; joy and gladness will be found in it,*
> *thanksgiving and* ***the voice of melody.***

Having a heart of thanksgiving toward the Lord and the spirit of gratitude will always give in to the voice of melody. Throughout the Psalms, King David declares his praise in singing including: Psalm 7:17; 9:2,11;

18:49; 21:13; 27:6; 30:12; 33:2; 47:6-7; 57:7-9; 61:8; 66:2; 68:4,32, and many more. David was surely in tune with God's heart.

We must meditate on the words of God because He is good and His mercy endures forever. This gives our songs content or another word I like to use is "texture." The definition of the word "texture" is the feel, appearance, or consistency of a surface or a substance. Every song has a feel and appearance to the imagination of the hearer and to the one who releases the song.

Songs come from the breath of the heart. God's creative word gives substance to our songs. We can sing His words and His mighty acts back to Him, reminding Him how good He is and how much we love Him. During our worship of Him, we go from the voice of melody to the voice of the Lord.

God's creative word gives substance to our songs.

Colossians 3:16 says:

> *"Let the word of Christ dwell in you richly in all wisdom, teaching and admonishing one*

another in psalms and hymns and spiritual songs, singing with grace in your hearts to the Lord.

God uses songs to teach us His principals, which help us understand His ways. It is like when you were taught the alphabet and your parents sang it to you repeatedly until the day you were able to recognize the letters by sight and sound them out to read. Songs we sing to the Lord or to others about God can teach us who He is. We are commanded to let the Word of God dwell richly in us. There must be some repetition at work in memorizing God's Word so that it can be written on the tablets of our hearts. This will help us know His voice from the voice of the stranger who may seek to do us harm.

*What then shall we say, brothers and sisters? When you come together, **each of you has a hymn, or a word of instruction, a revelation**, a tongue or an interpretation. Everything must be done **so that the church may be built up*** (1 Corinthians 14:26).

Your song or psalm will build up the church. Meditation upon the Word of the Lord is key to God's Word dwelling richly within our hearts, which produces new, spontaneous songs to the Lord and the Spirit of the Lord releases revelation to us.

> *Then what am I to do? I will pray with the spirit [by the Holy Spirit that is within me] and I will pray with the mind [using words I understand];* **I will sing with the spirit [by the Holy Spirit that is within me] and I will sing with the mind [using words I understand]** (1 Corinthians 14:15 AMP).

Singing in the Spirit and singing with understanding will help you and strengthen your inner self. When we do this, we are quickened by the Holy Spirit. God can give the psalmist insight. David said that the *"Spirit of the Lord spoke by me and His word was on his tongue"* (2 Samuel 23:2). This is a one way we develop the tongue of the learned.

Isaiah 50:4 says:

> **The Lord God has given Me the tongue of the learned**, *that I should know how to speak a word in season to him who is weary. He awakens Me morning by morning, He awakens My ear to hear as the learned.*

The benefits of singing in the spirit enhances our understanding of the heart and mysteries of God. When God puts His Word on our tongue, He his imparting wisdom. Prophetic singing can profit even the unbeliever.

> *But if an unbeliever or an inquirer comes in while everyone is prophesying, they are convicted of sin and are brought under judgment by all, as the secrets of their hearts are laid bare. So they will fall down and worship God, exclaiming, "God is really among you!"* (1 Corinthians 14:24-25)

The Spirit of God convinces and convicts people's hearts to worship the God of their salvation. Prophetic worship will cause people to see God. It is God's Word that discerns our hearts. Most of us who have experienced God's presence in this way know that only God could know the secrets of our hearts in such a powerful, provoking way that we are persuaded that God truly exists.

Davidic worshippers, or true worshippers, sing the song of the Lord. Hearing the song of the Lord being sung over me was glorious and life-changing, but to sing the songs of the Lord myself was like Heaven. It was not about how well I could sing. I was simply functioning as a true worshipper. I understood that the Spirit of the Lord was inside me.

And my worship provoked new and spontaneous songs to the Lord.

Flow Like a River

The more I worshipped, the more the Lord would fill my heart with joy. And then the songs began to flow like a river. Singing new songs can be like an endless river that flows from the spirit of a true worshipper, bringing a new refreshing every time.

Rivers can symbolize the supernatural. The Holy Spirit in us, is the supernatural power of God working from within the believer. The first time I spoke in tongues I was attending a prophetic service, and I instantly began to sing in tongues. It amazes me that I sang in the Spirit

God is always doing something new.

before I spoke with tongues. No one prayed for me to be filled with the Spirit; this infilling came upon me while I worshipped in the presence of the Lord.

Jesus says in John 7:38 (NIV), *"Whoever believes in me, as Scripture has said, rivers of living water will flow from within them."* That's right you have living waters flowing from within you. That is supernatural!

Ezekiel 47:9,12 describes a powerful river and how everything that flows from it or into it will have life and more abundantly—this is no ordinary river. This is the water of the Spirit. The same water that Jesus told the woman at the well she must drink (John 4:10,13-14).

The song of the Lord is like this river. Prophetic worship is a river! Picture a continual flow of the freshness of God's Spirit from where new things flow. God is always doing something new. And we must be willing to be part of His plan. I have seen how prophetic worship comes in a service and pushes dead and dry moves out from among the church and shifts God's people into present truth.

God says in Isaiah 43:19 (AMP), *""Listen carefully, I am about to do a new thing, now it will spring forth; will you not be aware of it? I will even put a road in the wilderness, rivers in the desert."*

Sometimes our lives can feel like a desert place. There are times in our worship services when it feels like nothing is moving. But the moment when the voice of the

Lord is released, the heavens drop down. God's voice is His presence.

> The earth shook, **the heavens dropped at the presence of God**: *even Sinai itself was moved at the presence of God, the God of Israel* (Psalm 68:8 KJV).

The Hebrew word *nataph* means to drop, drip, discourse. Strong's Exhaustive Concordance defines it as dropping, prophesy. A primitive root, to ooze i.e. Distill gradually, by implication, to fall in drops, figuratively, to speak by inspiration, drop(ping), prophesy(et).

Prophetic worship drops, *nataph*, down in our services and changes everything. When this happens, you will know the difference, because His presence is weighty. I am a seer and often when God comes into the worship service, I can see His hand moving over the congregation, doing whatever is needed. The Spirit of God will *nataph*, drop on me, and I will sing what the Lord is revealing to me at that time.

Hallelujah!

Chapter 6

SUPERNATURAL HEALINGS AND SONGS

*T*he following are some of the many miracles I have witnessed that were a result of God's goodness and grace.

I once was ministering the song of the Lord in a worship service and a woman received healing from crippling arthritis in her hands. I saw her hands, which were previously in an almost balled-up, fist condition, begin to stretch out and become normal.

Another time, while singing the song of the Lord in a church in Amsterdam, a 10-year-old little girl who was blind in one eye since birth was walked to the altar by her mom. She testified that while the song of Lord was being released, her daughter received full sight. In that same service many people received healing from blindness and other eye diseases.

Another lady was in a wheelchair for many years because of various complications from spinal injuries. She could not get up out of her chair or walk to altar. After hearing the song of the Lord, she was healed.

> *Sing a new song unto the Lord all the earth!*

I could testify for hours about the miracles that have taken place while prophetic worship and new songs were being released. When God's presence drops down into a service, He wants to do something big. Things we can't do in our own strength. Miracles, signs, and wonders. New things happen when His glory is released. Don't settle for less; yield to the voice of the Lord; sing unto the Lord a new song. Sing unto the Lord all the earth!

When we sing new songs, life begins to flow and everyone who partakes of it will be refreshed and renewed. New songs are different from learned songs, although learned songs are good and have their place in our personal and public ministry. New songs are commanded by God.

> *They **sing the song of Moses**, the servant of God, and **the song of the Lamb**, saying: "Great and marvelous are Your works, Lord God Almighty! Just and true are Your ways, O King of the saints!" (Revelation 15:3)*

We see from this verse in Revelation 15 that the people sang the song of Moses from Exodus 15. These were the ones who overcame the beast. This was their victory song. This can be considered as an *old* song. When Moses and the children of Israel were delivered from the hands of the Egyptians, they lifted their song up to Him because God had delivered them from their enemies.

In Psalm 40:1-3, David declared:

> *I waited patiently for the Lord; and He inclined to me, and heard my cry. He also brought me up out of a horrible pit, out of the miry clay, and set my feet upon a rock, and established my steps. **He has put a new song in my***

> **mouth**—*praise to our God; many will see it and fear, and will trust in the Lord.*

David's gratitude toward God released a new song and out of this song we see David's revelation of what God will do for the person who waits upon the Lord and walks in the fear of the Lord. The new song has redemptive power. Those who sing new songs help display the freshness of God's Spirit and what He is doing *now*. This power increases faith in God's ability to save and deliver us no matter what and when perils may come our way. Believers cannot help but notice a change in themselves and the atmosphere around them.

One of my first encounters with the glory of His presence, which I call my "Psalm 40 experience," happened in my dining room. I sat in the center of the floor and abandoned myself in worship until the presence of the Lord filled my house. And in that moment, it felt like a window was open to me. I noticed that my perception of God and other things became very clear. And everything I could not do in my own strength became easy.

The Birthday Song

The prophetic life of a believer can be very interesting and educational—but most of all life-changing. On my thirtieth birthday, I was awakened by the presence of the Lord. I looked around and noticed that everything looked bright and the television was in static mode. As I continued to look around, I noticed that my face was to the floor. In the midst of all that, I could see my room was filling up with peace and I was at the feet of Jesus. As much as I wanted to lift my head to see His face, I could not. I felt so overwhelmed with His presence, although I could only see a little past His ankles.

Nothing could have prepared me for what I heard next.

Jesus' voice was pure, peaceful, and genuine. I cannot find the words to describe the weightiness of His voice. The words He sang puzzled me; first of all, Jesus was singing to *me!* I went through waves of unbelief that Jesus would do such thing—to come into my room and sing to me. His song made me feel as if I was fading away into eternity.

The words He sang were very simple, "Ooo, just a little bit of something I give to you!"

I said, "Who?"

Jesus repeated the words a second time, ""Ooo, just a little bit of something I give to you!"

I said, "Who?"

The third time He sang it so convincingly that before I could get the word "Who" out, I perceived that the Lord was talking to me and singing His version of the Happy Birthday song to me.

Psalm 8:4 (NIV) says, *"What is mankind that you are mindful of them, human beings that you care for them?"* When the Lord sang over me a simple but beautiful and powerful song, I realized that God was thinking of me on my thirtieth birthday.

When God is mindful of us it means that He pays close attention to everything in our lives. All our concerns, purpose, and our destiny. No one can escape the eyes of God. It feels good when people celebrate your birthday. They remember your birthday by giving gifts, cards, etc. But when Jesus sings His birthday song to you, it is the best gift and blessing you can ever imagine.

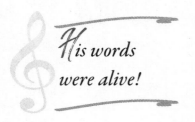

His words were alive!

I felt special and was in awe of Him—His words were alive to me. Jesus knew what my heart needed. One of greatest lessons I have learned as a prophetic psalmist is that Jesus' voice did not sound like the King James version of the Bible. I don't know why I was looking for the thee's and thou's, but they weren't in His song to me.

When I open my mouth to sing new songs I don't worry about translations. The Holy Spirit gives me what to sing. He has cultivated the words that come from the heart of God, which are for anyone to hear and understand. God wants to commune with humankind, His children. I totally depend on the Holy Spirit because He knows what is best—He knows what the world needs to hear.

After Jesus sang me the birthday song, the next overwhelming desire I had was to proclaim that God is real, true, and living. I understand why David declared to God in Psalm 84:10 (NIV) that "Better is one day in your courts than a thousand elsewhere." There was no place I wanted to be more than in the presence of the Lord. This became my new life, and I was transforming in the glory of the Lord.

Prophetic singing transforms the Church. We can sing new songs in our personal devotion time and in the congregation. *Prophetic ministry* is given to the Church to help build and perfect the saints. *Prophetic worship* functions the same way.

Chapter 7

JESUS SINGS

*M*ost believers do not believe that Jesus is singing in the midst of the Church. But I know that Jesus is our prototype in all areas of Christian living, which makes Him an excellent example for congregational worship. He sings in the midst of the congregation to His Father.

Jesus sings through us to His Father. Christ is inside believers. We must yield ourselves to His voice and release His praise in the congregation.

As Hebrews 2 and Psalm 22 say, we are to declare God's name within the assembly of His people. Hebrews 2:12 (NIV) says, *"I will declare your name to my brothers and sisters; in the assembly I will sing your praises."* And Psalm 22:22 (NIV) says, *"I will declare your name to my people; in the assembly I will praise you."*

Jesus is not a stranger to worshipping in the congregation of friends. In Matthew 26:30 He is found singing hymns with His disciples. Mark 14:26 also records this time when Jesus sang, *"When they had sung a hymn, they went out to the Mount of Olives."*

Jesus is our Chief Musician and Psalmist. In the tabernacle of David, David delivered songs to his chief musicians to be played or sung a particular way. They were the prophets who prophesied on the instruments. As we yield ourselves to the voice of the Lord, we can see that from the beginning Jesus is our Chief, the true Master of song. He is the Chief Prophet and global Worship Leader. He is in the midst of true worshippers praising our Father in every nation of the world.

Prophetic worship is our doorway to cross-culture worship. It breaks the barriers of cultures that focus solely on human traditions and advances the Kingdom of God. I believe prophetic worship is a key to eliminating racism in the Church. If we are going to be prophetic people, we will see that yielding ourselves to the voice of God leaves no room for racism, hate, or discrimination. Jesus died for every nation—the soul of all people. He died so that all people could worship the true and living God.

Prophetic worship breaks all barriers.

Prophetic worship can be used as a measuring rod in local churches. If leaders want to see the glory of God and souls coming into the Kingdom, there can be no place for the enemy. Leaders who yield themselves to the voice of God in prophetic worship want to see all nationalities worshipping together.

> ***The words of the prophets are in agreement*** *with this, as it is written: "After this I will return and rebuild David's fallen tent. Its ruins I will rebuild, and I will restore it, that* ***the rest of mankind may seek the Lord, even all the Gentiles*** *who bear my name, says the Lord, who does these things"* (Acts 15:15-17 NIV).

The Tabernacle of David is a blueprint for the Kingdom Church. One of the strongest characteristics of Davidic worship is the Spirit of prophecy. David wanted all to come to know and worship the true and living God. Jesus is our Greater David. He gave His life for all they are free to choose to serve the Lord and have eternal life.

Prophetic Worship Is Governmental

Prophetic worship is governmental. When David established twenty-four-hour worship and prayer, he was following a pattern that was in Heaven. Jesus instructed the disciples to pray that what is in Heaven is to be established upon the earth (Matthew 6:9-13). The governments of God's Kingdom would be established on earth through the praises and prayers of the saints.

Psalm 22:3 (KJV) says, *"But thou art holy, O thou that inhabitest the praises of Israel."* The New International Version puts it this way: *"Yet you* [God] *are enthroned as the Holy One; you are the one Israel praises."* The throne of God would be manifested upon the praises of Israel and the governments of Heaven would release God's judgments upon the earth. God's view of earth would elaborately be established as it is in Heaven through righteous prayers and righteous judgments.

> *Praise the Lord! Sing to the Lord a new song, and His praise in the assembly [congregation] of saints* (Psalm 149:1).

Psalm 149:6-9 says:

> **Let the high praises of God be in their mouth**, *and a two-edged sword in their hand, to execute vengeance on the nations, and punishments on the peoples; to bind their kings with chains, and their nobles with fetters of iron; to execute on them the written judgment—this honor have all His saints. Praise the Lord!*

Most believers do not know how powerful their combined prayers and worship can be. My first experience in praise, prayer, and worship was in our mid-week prayer gathering. I remember going around asking other saints, "Is there such a thing as worship intercession?" Our lead intercessor taught us to worship and pray the Word.

I attended a worship conference in Dallas, Texas, called the International Worship Institution under the leadership of Lamar Bushman—and there it was, the answer to my question. Worship Intercession was one of the classes taught at the conference. God was confirming to me the power of Heaven's governments being established on earth through the prayers and worship of the saints.

Revelation 5:8-9 tells us:

> *Now when He had taken the scroll, the four living creatures and the twenty-four elders fell down before the Lamb,* **each having a harp**, *and* **golden bowls** *full of incense, which are* **the prayers of the saints**. *And* **they sang a new song**, *saying: "You are worthy to take the scroll, and to open its seals; for* **You were slain, and have redeemed us to God by Your blood** *out of every tribe and tongue and people and nation.*

The redeemed of Lord have the *honor* to sing new songs and prayers that stir up the righteous judgments of God because of the blood of the Lamb and His resurrection power.

I believe David saw a glimpse of this when he established twenty-four-hour worship around the throne. Those who would worship around the clock in David's tabernacle would offer up petitions and giving thanks to the Lord.

A Prophetic View

In prophetic view of this, many years ago the Lord gave me a picture of a nation of people who would have rule in the heavens and the earth through prayer and worship. No enemy would be able to penetrate the skies above us or the earth beneath us and around us. He gave me images of a military regime, not the armies of the world but angels and the prayers and worship charging to the earth. I could see that all things in Heaven and earth would be governed by prayer. We are God's kings and priests who would rule with Him.

> *Sing to the Lord a new song, and his praise from the ends of the earth, you who go down to the sea, and all that is in it, you islands, and all who live in them. Let the wilderness and its towns raise their voices; let the settlements where Kedar lives rejoice. Let the people of Sela sing for joy; let them shout from the mountaintops. Let them give glory to the Lord and proclaim his praise in the islands. The Lord will march out like a champion, like a warrior he will stir up his zeal; with a shout he will raise the battle cry and will triumph over his enemies* (Isaiah 42:10-13 NIV).

During prophetic worship, the Lord will break out in new songs of war, prophetic shouting, dancing, and declarations that release His strength and power against our enemies. We must yield to the Lord so that He may use His body to say, sing, preach, dance, and prophesy His might throughout the land.

Prophetic praise and worship cause us to prosper.

Jehoshaphat told the people that if they believed in the Lord God and believe His prophets, they shall prosper. Wow! What a word. After this powerful word of encouragement and hope, he appoints the singers.

> *And when he had consulted with the people, he appointed those who should **sing to the Lord, and who should praise the beauty of holiness**, as they went out before the army and were saying: **"Praise the Lord, for His mercy endures forever."** Now **when they began to sing and to praise, the Lord set ambushes** against the people of Ammon, Moab, and Mount Seir, who had come against Judah; **and they were defeated** (2 Chronicles 20:21-22).*

God's prophetic instructions to Jehoshaphat caused him to prosper against his enemies. Prophetic praise and worship acts as spiritual warfare. God governs and rule over our enemies with this kind of praise.

Prophetic Praise Releases Power

Numbers 21:17-18 (NIV) says:

> *Then **Israel sang this song: "Spring up, O well! Sing about it,** about the well that the princes dug, that the nobles of the people sank— the nobles with scepters and staffs." Then they went from the wilderness to Mattanah,*

Israel sang this prophetic praise song to the well that God miraculously provided water for. If God was with them in providing supernatural water in the past, He would surely be with them again. Oh, if the well could tell the tale of past and future victories! Oh well, do prophesy!

Praise by nature is prophetic. Every believer can offer God unrehearsed spontaneous praise, because God is worthy. We praise God and worship Him until the glory falls.

Chapter 8

THE PROPHETIC FLOW

⁓

Many minstrels and psalmists who have never experienced prophetic worship have a hard time understanding what it means to get into a "prophetic flow." The reality is, if they have not been taught about the prophetic and the roles of minstrels and psalmists in worship, this is going to be difficult. I have been operating in this dimension for more than twenty years, and I tell you it gets more glorious as I grow in intimacy and knowledge and understanding.

Knowledge and understanding are keys to functioning in this type of ministry. I teach that we are to bring our lifestyle to the platform. We don't have to try to *make* something happen if we truly have a lifestyle of prayer, praise, and worship. The platform can be intimidating; I have heard many ask, "How can you encourage a prophetic flow in a forty-five-minute or more Sunday morning service?" My answer: "The Holy Spirit is our Helper, and working with the pastor secures our ability and liberty to flow."

When leading worship in different churches or trying to implement a new worship environment in your own church, yes, this type of change needs permission from the church or ministry leadership. This approval helps break the restrictions off your mind and gives you the ability to govern your environment in an orderly fashion. Teaching, training, and activating is important. Everyone needs to be prepared for the glory. This is one form of practicing His presence.

There are many reasons why it is difficult to get into a prophetic flow, or musical flow. This could be a language or phrase that is not commonly used in certain churches or denominations. Some leaders may feel they are losing control. Maybe you have a song list that you are used to and that can be a one issue between you and the leaders. It is okay not to use the list and allow the Holy Spirit to lead you into a new song. We must be courageous and forget about the looks on the faces of people who are accustomed to the old ways. Leaders are instrumental in helping develop a prophetic culture in the local house.

I know it can be a little scary and challenging when you are trying to introduce

It is God's idea and desire to have a prophetic people.

something new. But remember, Davidic worship is an essential part of the well-being of the Church. Acts 15 tells us that God is restoring David's Tabernacle. David created praise and worship from a deep desire to please God and a heavenly pattern that was given him by God. Those who desire to be prophetic people or Church must understand that it is God's idea and desire to have a prophetic people.

Psalm 69:30-31 (NIV) tells us:

> *"I will praise God's name in song and glorify him with thanksgiving. This will please the*

> *Lord more than an ox, more than a bull with its horns and hooves.*

And Acts 15:16-17 says:

> *After this I will return and will rebuild the tabernacle of David, which has fallen down; I will rebuild its ruins, and I will set it up; so that the rest of mankind may seek the Lord, even all the Gentiles who are called by My name, says the Lord who does all these things.*

In Acts 15, the Gentles are coming into a new covenant by grace. The nations of earth are invited to come and worship in David's tabernacle. God changes their nature and changes them into new people. Davidic worship is full of God's glory, and the glory will flow out of the individuals who live a lifestyle of praise, prayer, and prophetic worship.

Getting into a prophetic flow is yielding to the Holy Spirit and allowing Him to help make our praise glorious to our Lord. What does this look like? Minstrels and psalmists yield their gifts to God; they will worship God in Spirit and in truth. In the tabernacle of David, he commanded them to prophesy on the instruments.

When David commanded the psalmists and minstrels to prophesy, he was simply commanding them to worship God in Spirit and truth this was not about seeing how gifted and skilled they were; he knew that were skilled because he trained them along with their fathers. These leaders were committed to offering sacrifices of praise, prayer, and worship.

> *At this I fell at his feet to worship him. But he said to me, "Don't do that! I am a fellow servant with you and with your brothers and sisters who hold to the testimony of Jesus. Worship God! For it is **the Spirit of prophecy who bears testimony to Jesus**"* (Revelation 19:10 NIV).

David's command to the minstrels to prophesy on the instrument is best understood by looking at Revelation 19:10, the testimony of Jesus as the Spirit of prophecy. Christ is revealed the Spirit of God reveals the man Jesus to the worshipper and through the worshipper. An instrument cannot be prophetic, but can be used as tool. God's Spirit is resting upon the minstrel or psalmist. This is true worship whereby the voice of the Lord is released. Prophetic worship is a two-way conversation between

God and humans. I believe this a key for the knowledge of His glory to be revealed to all humankind.

> *David, together with the commanders of the army, set apart some of the sons of Asaph, Heman and Jeduthun for the ministry of prophesying, accompanied by harps, lyres and cymbals. Here is the list of the men who performed this service:* (1 Chronicles 25:1 NIV).

This is a heavenly pattern from the throne room of God. The 24-hour worship and prayer are a picture of a lifestyle a daily devotion, a way of living before the Lord. We must teach believers and those who are committed to service of prayer, praise, and worship the tools they need for cultivating this type of worship in our local church services.

David employed 8,000 Levites for service in his tabernacle for the Lord. Again, this is a prophetic picture of what he saw in Heaven. You might wonder how anyone today can get 8,000 believers to function under this type of ministry. Remember, all people are called to prayer, praise, and prophetic worship. We are kings and priests of the Lord. God desires His people to be prophetic.

The Bible tells us in Revelation 5:8-10 (NIV):

*And when he had taken it, the four living creatures and the twenty-four elders fell down before the Lamb. Each one had a harp and they were holding golden bowls full of incense, which are the prayers of God's people. And **they sang a new song**, saying: "You are worthy to take the scroll and to open its seals, because you were slain, and with your blood you purchased for God persons from every tribe and language and people and nation. **You have made them to be a kingdom and priests to serve our God, and they will reign on the earth**."*

We must teach and admonish believers what is pleasing to the Lord and create an environment that God can rest in. This is possible so that when we gather together to worship our King, all can be blessed. We should not make our worship encounters about us. We lift the desire of Jesus so all may know *Him*. He will draw the people into His presence, and with joy Zion will receive her King.

Chapter 9

BECOMING A PROPHETIC MINSTREL AND PSALMIST

My first experience with leading prophetic worship was very dramatic and literally almost traumatizing. I know you may be wondering, *How could leading worship be that dramatic?* The truth is, I didn't know what I was doing. I thought the singers were just singing. Don't get me wrong, I loved God and His presence, but I didn't understand worship leading and how to function in the local church. Surely it was a little different from how I would worship at home? Later, I discovered it was not much different at all, except for the additional singers, minstrels, and intercessors.

I walked to the podium and began singing something I don't remember, but I can say it was not a learned song. As I was singing, I immediately realized something different. I discerned that my voice was not enough, and my gift was failing me. I felt like everyone would laugh at me. I put the microphone down on the podium and began to walk backward toward the singers. I was afraid because I didn't understand the dynamics of leading. I was encouraged by the other singers to go back and finish.

The first thing I said was, "Jesus help me...I don't know what I'm doing." Suddenly I could feel the presence of Lord with me. My mind became clear and I could trust God. The atmosphere started to feel like my private times with Lord and I desired to flow where the Holy Spirit was leading me. My prophetic gift was activated in a way that was different from just singing spontaneous songs to the Lord.

My spiritual eyes were opened, and I trusted what Jesus was revealing to me in the service. I needed Him and wanted more of Him. He was filling my heart with His desire for us as we worshipped.

Then I saw a banner covering the ceiling: ABORTION. I asked Him, "What is that?" He impressed upon me to sing about life and that He came to bring us life more abundantly (John 10:10). I remember singing words to bind the spirit of abortion and then He prompted me to sing about my testimony, how many people were being set free—and I was a different woman.

The intercessors were praying, and I understood that they were a huge part of what God was doing in the room.

Humility, love, and grace filled my heart and I wanted nothing else. I knew that if I was going to be God's worship leader, I could not leave Him out of the equation. He is the Chief Psalmist and Minstrel. Jesus Himself was teaching me how to navigate in leading worship.

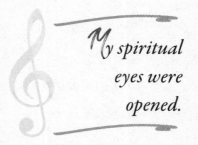

My spiritual eyes were opened.

The demonic spirit that was over the room was trying to get me to abort what God wanted to do in me and through me. Realizing that, in that moment God became my Defense and my Victor. Sharing my testimony in song was not a coincidence, it was God's strategy. He is perfect in war.

I went where He went and spoke what He said. My private times in the secret place became public and the Holy Spirit was the governor of my spirit as I yielded more and more to Him. That day I learned that when we lead worship, Jesus has much to say and do with us; He does not want us to just sing *about* Him—He wants to be sung to, and He wants to sing over His people. We must yield ourselves to His desire. He will not despise the humble. In fact, He lifts up those who humble themselves before Him (James 4:10).

> *Prophetic worship beings with a humble heart toward God.*

Becoming a prophetic psalmist and minstrel must began with a humble heart toward God. God will not dwell with pride and vanity. We must be filled with the Spirit of God; remember, He is our Helper. Spending time with God in the secret place is where we learn who we are in Christ Jesus. We learn how much God loves us. Here is where we develop trust in God and learn to know His voice. God wants to reveal His secrets and mysteries to us. Never leave this secret place; understand that there is no replacement for the glory.

When we dwell in the secret place, God will pour His oil of refreshment upon our lives. The oil is the anointing that destroys yokes. Allow God to heal your heart. Many gifted psalmists and minstrels have heart issues. Allow the miracle of healing to come upon your heart. God needs your heart to release His emotions through. This will help you convey the temperament of what God is doing as you minister before His people.

When we look at King David's life, we see that as a young man he spent quality time with the Lord while he took care of his father's sheep. He was ministering before the Lord out in the fields. He loved the Lord with all his heart and all he wanted to do was to be in God's presence all the days of his life.

God's truth must live in your heart.

We cannot minister effectively if we don't know our God. How can we minister His Word if we don't have truth abiding within our hearts? I don't think many people like the process of training and waiting, because they are driven by their lusts and desires. Every now and then we should ask ourselves what we are holding in our hearts—the Lord's truth or our selfishness.

David never sought fame for himself. When he was just a young boy he was sought out by the king. His reputation went before him as a skilled minstrel, an anointed minstrel; and because of his anointing, the king of Israel asked for him. This gives us something to think about. Out of all the musicians in Israel, David was the one called upon. Remember, he was not just called upon to minster at a sweet sixteen party, he was called upon by the king. The Bible says that King Saul loved David. I believe what we can take from this is we don't have to seek fame; God will make mention of our name in the courts of leaders. I believe the quickest way to be disqualified from this level of favor is to seek your own fame.

Psalm 27:4 tells us, *"One thing I have desired of the Lord, that will I seek: that I may dwell in the house of the Lord all the days of my life, to behold the beauty of the Lord and to inquire in His temple."*

And Psalm 84:10 (NIV) is worth repeating, *"Better is one day in your courts than a thousand elsewhere; I would rather be a doorkeeper in the house of my God than dwell in the tents of the wicked."*

The School of the Prophets

Personal devotion should be primary for all believers to desire and commit to daily. Again, having a gift to sing or play an instrument does not automatically qualify anyone for ministry of any kind. I strongly recommend developing a faithful devotion to the Lord. Some may disagree, but singers in the Bible waited upon their appointment; it was treated as an office. Today, we have hundreds of singers and minstrels, yet many are not in the service of the Lord.

> *And these are they whom David set over the service of song in the house of the Lord, after that the ark had rest. And they ministered before the dwelling place of the tabernacle of the congregation with singing, until Solomon had built the house of the Lord in Jerusalem: and then they waited on their office according to their order* (1 Chronicles 6:31-32 KJV).

The prophet Samuel was the overseer of the school of the prophets. This term can also mean the company of prophets. These prophets were Levites who were trained under Samuel the prophet. David spent much time training with Samuel. Minstrels and psalmists need training, preferably with prophets as it is beneficial to their growth and accountability. Prophets should be part of the worship department; they are instrumental in helping discern the flow of the Spirit and implement what God is doing in our local services. They are not limited to the local house, but play an important role in perfecting all the saints.

> *Chenaniah, leader of the Levites, was instructor in charge of the music, because he was skillful; …David was clothed with a robe of fine linen, as were all the Levites who bore the ark, the singers, and Chenaniah the music master with the singers. David also wore a linen ephod* (1 Chronicles 15:22,27).

Chenaniah ministered in the tabernacle of David; he was known as a prophet and also called the musical director, choir director, or captain over the Levite singers. The Bible says that he was skillful. The Young's Literal Translation of the Bible says, *"Chenaniah, head of the Levites, [is] over the burden; he instructed about the burden, for he [is] intelligent."*

God's Word translation of 1 Chronicles 15:22 says, *"Chenaniah, a Levite leader, instructed others how to sing prophetic songs because he was skilled at it."* And the Jubilee Bible 2000 translates, *"And Chenaniah, prince of the Levites in prophecy, for he presided in prophecy, because he had understanding."*

Most translations are very clear about Chenaniah's role as the one with a strong prophetic burden to release what

God is singing through the praise and the worship. He is also described as the planting of the Lord.

I believe this type of anointing will cause congregational worship to flourish and grow in the anointing and glory. Prophetic worship helps us navigate in the spirit realm. Many prophets are most concerned about the glory of God being released, and they want God to be revealed. Having prophets as part of the worship team can be exciting because they can detect the flow of God's will, desires, and intent.

Catch the wave—the flow of the Spirit!

Remember, the most important thing is that God wants all His people to be prophetic. I strongly dislike the taboo of moving in the prophetic realm. I believe true worship by nature is prophetic. I encourage my brothers and sisters to trust God and catch the wave of His Spirit.

Get in the flow!

Chapter 10

CONTENT AND CONTEXT

I like to use the word "content" to describe the level of God's Word that is within a person's heart and mind that can be used as a resource in daily living.

When I was a baby in Christ, I knew very little Scripture, but I began to grow in Word and truth by reading the Bible, His written Word. As I grew in a deeper relationship with God, more of His Word became engrafted within my heart. It became easier to discern my spirit apart from the Spirit of God, which is important in the dynamics of prophetic worship. The Word of God is a discerner, let's keep that in mind.

Speaking of the mind, as new creatures we have the mind of Christ; and in order to be perfected in the things of God, we must have a renewed mind. We cannot speak as God if we don't know His Word.

John 1:1 reveals that *"In the beginning was the Word and the Word was with God, and the Word was God."*

> *Study God's Word for a renewed mind.*

Prophetic people must understand the importance of the Word of God. We must make time to study God's Word and worship Him using His Word that it may abide in you, live in you, guide you daily. The Bible says that Jesus is the Word of God. He is a sure word of prophecy. We must have balance in our release of the prophetic—knowing God's Word brings balance in every area of life.

In the school of the prophets, Samuel taught the Word of God to the Levites; it was part of the training along with God's commandments. This is like new wine to many, but remember you can't put new wine in old wineskins. God is doing something new in worship and it's going to take a renewed mind and heart to flow with it. The new wine will cause an expansion, and this is what God is doing. He is expanding His Kingdom.

> *Let the word of Christ dwell in you richly in all wisdom, teaching and admonishing one another in psalms and hymns and spiritual songs, singing with grace in your hearts to the Lord* (Colossians 3:16).

We are commanded by the Word of God to let God's Word dwell richly in us. The word "richly" is defined as having full measure, amply. We are to be full of God's Word. When have a sound Word foundation, the Holy Spirit will have much to work with, or greater capacity to speak more accurately through a person's spirit. Keep in mind that God is not contrary to His own Word; He cannot lie.

Most people have not grasped the fact that teaching takes place during praise and worship. We are more accustomed to being encouraged during praise and worship. Biblically sound praise and worship helps us to know God. God reveals Himself and His heart and plans through His Word. We are to praise and worship God with understanding.

Speaking prophetic words as well as singing the prophecy require the same principles in action.

Context

I believe that apostolic and prophetic churches may focus a little more on context than other denominations where prophecy is rare. Churches that are team-oriented will focus on the biblical principles of knowing in part. Yes, the Bible says we know "in part," also this means that more than one person can speak or sing what God is saying; although more than one person may speak or sing prophetically, no one is speaking out of context. We can judge ourselves and submit to the Holy Spirit's work in the room in the context in which He is speaking.

First Corinthians 14:32 says that *"the spirits of the prophets are subject to the prophets."* We are subject, or submitted, to each other; and more than anything, we have the responsibility of governing our own spirits.

The apostle Paul reminds the Corinthians and us that, "For we know in part and we prophesy in part. ...For you can all prophesy one by one, that all may learn and all may be encouraged" (1 Corinthians 13:9; 14:31).

I believe when we have order in anything, we will have peace. The prophetic can seem to some that it's out of control. Organized churches wonder, "What in Heaven's name are you prophets doing?" They have a sense of dread because they think they are losing control. They don't know how to react when God takes over.

Truthfully, many prophets have given the prophetic a bad reputation because they abuse this powerful gift. I say that receiving a prophetic word is not something you control; it must be governed first by the person who is prophesying; submit yourself the Holy Spirit and the traditions of the church leadership where you are attending and or ministering. The Holy Spirit is such a gentleman; He will not force you into the prophetic.

Be encouraged through prophecy.

We are to be encouraged through prophecy. God wants all His people to prophesy. We cannot ignore the wonders that take place when God uses music to prophesy. Music is a powerful tool. Every generation will prophesy through their music. Yes, music is in the voice of God.

I cannot express enough about this powerful gift we have been given by our loving Father. Did you know that your voice can be music to someone's ears? You don't need an instrument to make music. Practice creating melodies in heart and you will see the power in your own voice.

Babies love to hear the tone of their mother and father's voice because they recognize the sound that is produced from their loving parents. As God's children, we should recognize and appreciate the sound of our heavenly Father's voice. When we as a body of believers know how to operate in the fullness of this powerful gift of music and prophecy, we will see more people absorbing it as a way of life, a lifestyle of prophetic worship. Not a few, but *all* people will be singing to the Lord and singing as God to His children.

11

PROPHETIC WORSHIP NUGGETS

*T*he following are important nuggets of God's wisdom pulled from His Word that summarizes all that I pray touched your heart and spirit as you read. May you take with you the truth of the dynamics of prophetic worship and put into practice what you have learned to reach a deeper level of relationship with God the Father.

- Prophetic worship is key to staying fresh. Many believers strive to stay current in the latest worship trends—but what is more important than being trendy is Spirit-filled worship. (John 4:23-24)

- Jesus is the central focal point of true worship. There is no one above Him. To engage the supernatural realm of prophetic worship, He must be lifted up above all names. (John 12:32)

- Prophetic worship is not limited to singing only. We can express the heart and mind of God through dance and other art forms. Our God, Elohim, is the Creator of Heaven and earth. In the book of Genesis, we see the earth as a blank canvas; God by His Spirit, paints with His words and His breath and gives dominion to us. (Psalm 150:1-6; Exodus 15:20)

- Prophetic worship will break churches and denominations out of traditional and cultural worship. It is a model for all of God's people globally. (Acts 15:15-17)

- Prophetic worship requires true and complete trust in God. To release what God is speaking and or saying, the Holy Spirit helps us say what needs to be said. Have faith! (Psalm 81:10)

- Prophetic worship is not just for the pastor and key leaders. Develop a habit of prophesying. Practice! (1 Samuel 10:2-5)

- Get around some prophetic people. It is contagious. You will prophesy! (1 Samuel 19:21)

- Prophetic worship allows the Church, the Lord's bride, to sing love songs to Jesus, the Bridegroom, in the midst of His people. Jesus loves love songs and sings over us with His love. Songs of the bride display the beauty of God's love toward His people, His bride.

(Song of Solomon 1:2, 5:16, 8:6-7; Zephaniah 3:17)

- Prayer is essential for a strong prophetic anointing. It is another way and one of the most important ways we communicate with God—prayer, worship, and prophecy. King David is a prototype for minstrels and psalmists. David's lifestyle of prayer and intercession is key to the anointing that was on his life. We don't talk much about his prayer life; however, it is worth the attention and demonstration as to how God will anoint your devotion. Refer to Revelation 5:8, which is called harp (worship) and bowl (prayers).

- David's success is a result of his face-to-face ministry to the Lord and desire to seek the Lord all the days of his life. I have found that individuals and churches that have a constant flow of prophetic rivers have a strong desire to seek after God. The prophetic streams flow from the head to all auxiliaries—

even the children prophesy. (Psalm 27:4)

- Many leaders fear operating in prophetic worship, or any kind of prophetic ministry, because they feel they will lose control. Prophetic ministry is not something you can control. It has to be governed by mature leadership and is designed by God to perfect the saints. (Ephesians 4:11-16)

Conclusion

A PROPHETIC WORD

I believe that the untapped power of music and prophecy is ready to hit the earth. The Lord spoke this prophetic word to me two years ago concerning prophetic psalmists and minstrels going out into world. He said:

> I will send My prophetic psalmists and minstrels into the world. The world needs

sweet psalmists like David. But not all will be qualified to go, because they desire the world and fame...it is no longer about making My name great to them.

I want to heal the brokenhearted through the pure sound of My voice. I will heal the spirit of insanity and confusion off My people. Those who have said there is no hope, I will bring hope through My songs. I will sing over My chosen people, those predestined to know Me, and quiet them with My love and protection. I will arise in a new sound over the nations— many will hear the new sound and run under My protection.

I will release a consuming fire of My love that will burn in the hearts of all people who have chased after Me.

I have been purifying vessels! This time they will not be seduced by lies of the enemy. This new anointing that is coming will bring about sounds and wonders. I will judge the prideful sounds of music of those who produce but will not repent. I will breathe a fresh wind upon those who desire to hear My voice in the music that they produce.

The shouts of joy will bring down the walls of racism and paganism that plague the youth. The traps that the enemy has used to snare the youth I will pull the plug from their influences.

Trap music no more!

ABOUT KATHRYN SUMMERS

*K*athryn Summers is an ordained prophet, psalmist, and worship director at Crusaders Church under the leadership of Apostle John Eckhardt. Kathryn has ministered as a prophetic voice for more than twenty years and has traveled to more than thirty nations, teaching and activating local churches in the pattern of the Tabernacle of David.

Kathryn's desire is to see generations live out their prophetic mandate as Davidic people. Many believers have received miracles and healing as she released the song of the Lord.

Kathryn has several musical recordings and is the author of *The Dynamics of Prophetic Worship*. She resides in Chicago, Illinois.

The author can be contacted at
ksummersbooking@gmail.com.